WENTRI MERDIANI, MULYADI SUHARDI, & TUTI HARTATI

From Village to World

Bringka Coffee Technology and Innovation Assistance

Contents

CHAPTER 1. INTRODUCTION

1.1 Background

Village potential in community-based economic development.

According to Law of the Republic of Indonesia Number 41 of 2009 Article 1 Paragraph 8 concerning the protection of sustainable food agricultural land. Food agriculture is a human effort to manage land and agro-ecosystems with the help of technology, capital, labor, and management to achieve food sovereignty and security as well as people's welfare (Sunny, 2021:126). Based on the definition above, it can be concluded that the Agricultural Sector is an activity carried out by humans by utilizing biological resources as plant cultivation or farming to produce food or energy sources and to manage their environment. Coffee plants are included in the agricultural sector which is generally cultivated in rural areas.

In Indonesia, the agricultural sector in the broad sense is divided into five sub-sectors, including (Sattar, 2018:127) :

1. Food crops. Food crops are often referred to as the people's agricultural subsector which includes food commodities such as: rice, corn, sweet potatoes, peanuts, soybeans, vegetables and fruits.
2. Plantations are divided into two, namely:
3. People's plantations are plantations that are managed by the people themselves on a small scale with simple technology. The crops produced are: rubber, corporal, tea, coffee, tobacco, cloves, cotton, chocolate and spices.
4. Large plantations are plantation activities run by companies with legal

status. The crops produced are: rubber, tea, coffee, palm oil, chocolate, quinine, sugar cane and various fibers.

5. Forestry. Forest products consist of three activities, namely:
6. Logging produces logs, firewood, charcoal and bamboo.
7. Other forest products include rattan, wood resin, tree bark, roots and tubers.
8. Livestock. This subsector includes the production of large and small livestock such as: eggs, fresh milk, wool, and animal slaughter products.

Fisheries. This subsector includes all results of marine fisheries activities, public waters, ponds, fish farms, rice fields and cages.

Farming is a science that studies how someone allocates existing resources effectively and efficiently to obtain high profits at a certain time. It is said to be effective if farmers can allocate the resources they have as well as possible, and it can be said that efficient use of these resources produces output that exceeds input (Yusriadi and Irninthya, 2022) . Furthermore, it is explained that the entrepreneur himself or the science of farming is to investigate the methods of a farmer as an entrepreneur in compiling, organizing and running the company (Nur Zaman, et al. 2021).

Farmer groups are groups of people who are a unity with identity and customs in a system of norms that regulate patterns and regulate interactions between people. Regulation of the Minister of Agriculture, number: 273/KPTS/OT.160/4/2007, dated April 13, concerning the development of farmer institutions, states that farmer groups are defined as groups of farmers, livestock breeders, plantations formed on the basis of similar environmental conditions and familiarity to improve and develop member businesses. The main function of farmer groups is basically as a vehicle for the teaching and learning process, a vehicle for cooperation, and a vehicle for production. Farming is a livelihood in the form of farming. Thus, farmer groups are groups of people who have activities in the form of farming who live together as a unity with identity and interaction with fellow normative systems that apply in them. Farmer groups are characterized by knowing each other, being familiar and trusting each other among members, having the same views and interests in farming and having similarities in traditions or settlements, business areas, types of businesses, economic or social status, language, education and also there is a division of tasks and responsibilities among members based on mutual agreement. The purpose of the farmer group is to form a farmer association that functions as a medium for extension which is expected to be more focused on changing farming activities for the better. Better farming activities can be seen from the increase in farming productivity which in turn will increase farmers' income so that it will support the creation of better welfare for farmers and their families. However, many people still assume that farmer groups do not have a role in increasing income for farmers. Farmer group development needs to be carried out more intensively, directed and planned so that it can increase its role and function. (Professor of IPB, 2021).

Four potential forms of farmer groups in contributing to economic development, namely as follows (Amruddin, et al. 2022) :

1. The expansion of other economic sectors is highly dependent on output growth in the agricultural sector, both from the demand side as a source of continuous food supply following population growth, and from the supply side as a source of raw materials for production needs in other sectors such as manufacturing and trade.
2. Agriculture serves as an important source of growth in domestic demand for products from other sectors of the economy.
3. As a source of capital for investment in other economic sectors.
4. As an important source of trade balance surplus (source of foreign exchange) both through exports of agricultural products and by increasing agricultural production or by increasing domestic agricultural production to replace imports.

Based on government regulations, village governance is defined as the administration of government affairs and the interests of the local community in the government system of the Unitary State of the Republic of Indonesia (Law of the Republic of Indonesia number 6. Year 2014 Article 1 paragraph 2

). This Law outlines the authority of the village in various aspects, including in development planning, village financial management, community services, and implementation of development programs. In addition, this Law emphasizes that the administration of Village Government, implementation of development, community development, and community empowerment are based on Pancasila, the 1945 Constitution of the Republic of Indonesia, the Unitary State of the Republic of Indonesia, and Bhinneka Tunggal Ika. This Law regulates material on the Principles of Regulation, Position and Types of Villages, Village Arrangement, Village Authority, Implementation of Village Government, Rights and Obligations of Villages and Village Communities, Village Regulations, Village Finances and Village Assets, Village Development and Development of Rural Areas, Village-Owned Enterprises, Village Cooperation, Village Community Institutions and Village Customary Institutions, as well as Guidance and Supervision.

Building a Sustainable Village: Understanding and Implementing Community-Based Creative Economy Strengthening is an important key in supporting sustainable development in the village. Strengthening the community-based creative economy not only improves the economy, but also preserves the environment and strengthens cultural values.

Community-based creative economy involves the use of creativity, innovation, and local knowledge to produce products, services, or experiences that have economic value. The creative economy has great potential for empowering rural communities, increasing income, and preserving cultural heritage. In addition, the creative economy also encourages innovation, job creation, and village infrastructure development. Strengthening the community-based creative economy is not just about business capital, but also includes developing human resource capacity, mentoring, and creating a supportive ecosystem.

Community-based creative economy development is one of the important pillars in building a sustainable village. One of the crucial steps in this development is identifying local potential that is the basic capital for developing the creative economy. A sustainable village is not only about physical development, but also about economic empowerment. And this is where the community-based creative economy comes into play. By utilizing local potential, villages can create new economic opportunities, while preserving their cultural heritage.

Citizen engagement is essential to building a successful creative ecosystem. Villagers must feel ownership of creative economy projects and see how they can contribute.

Involve residents in the planning process and give them the opportunity to share ideas and thoughts. Encourage collaboration between local artists and businesses, and provide a space for them to interact and learn from each other. In this way, the village can unleash its collective creativity and realize ideas that truly reflect their identity and aspirations.

The role of coffee as a local leading commodity.

One of the agriculture that can drive the development of social and economic welfare is coffee plantation farmers. It can be said that coffee is a superior commodity because its market opportunities are quite good in domestic and foreign trade (export). Coffee commodities in Indonesia have an important role as a source of non-oil and gas foreign exchange for the country from the agricultural sector. Indonesia is the fourth largest coffee producer in the world, so there is a great opportunity for each region to manage environmental assets as a source of economic drivers.

Many regions in Indonesia have coffee plantations and their own unique processing methods. The resulting flavors and characteristics are very diverse and make Indonesian coffee products increasingly popular, both among local and international communities. In 2022, Indonesian coffee plantations reached 1.29 million hectares or an increase of 0.5 percent compared to the previous year which reached 1.28 million hectares. The majority of coffee plantations in Indonesia are smallholder plantations, namely 1.26 hectares (ha). Meanwhile, large-scale coffee plantations managed by the state and private sector amount to 23,200 ha.

In addition to its production being consumed domestically, Indonesian coffee production is also exported to other countries including the United States, Egypt, Germany, and Malaysia. Most of Indonesia's coffee exports

(80 percent) consist of robusta beans, and the rest of arabica beans. As a plantation commodity, coffee exports are the fourth largest foreign exchange earner for Indonesia after palm oil, rubber and cocoa.

As a leading commodity for the domestic plantation sector, the coffee industry plays a crucial role in national economic growth. The coffee industry has contributed as a driver of coffee farmers' income, a source of foreign exchange, a producer of industrial raw materials, and a provider of jobs through processing, marketing, and export and import trade activities.

For example, to maximize the potential of the coffee industry, the Government continues to support improvements in upstream governance, farmer institutional governance, and post-harvest governance in order to increase productivity, *brands,* and packaging standards in order to enter the global market. One of the coffee farmers in Indonesia is Palintang coffee in Bandung Regency, which initially aimed to preserve the forest and then developed to build the welfare of farmers in the Mount Palintang area, Cipanjalu Village and Girimekar Village, Cilengkrang District, Bandung Regency. Based on the data found, there are currently 130 people who have joined the forest farmer group in the Mount Pelintang area. Pelintang coffee is also marketed in Bandung, Jakarta, Kutai, Surabaya, and Bali and has also succeeded in penetrating the international market in a number of countries, including Sweden, Japan, and Malaysia (Posmedia Journal, 2018). The Farmer Group which was founded in 1999 initially only tried to plant coffee in the forest area, then produced a harvest and then expanded the coffee planting to 50 hectares by a man named Pak Amin. From this personal experiment, the Coffee Farmers group was formed and began to be known by the community in 2005. The main objective of the Palintang Coffee Farmers group was initially to maintain the sustainability of the forest around Mount Palintang and in its development aimed to improve the economic welfare of farmers in the Mount Palintang area, Cipanjalu Village, Cilengkrang District, Bandung Regency.

During 2017 to 2022, the development of Palintang coffee harvest in Bandung Regency produced around 50 to 60 tons per harvest which was gradual every 5 months (Posmedia Journal, 2018). In practice, these farmers process coffee in three ways, namely 1) natural, 2) *honey* (semi wash), and 3) *full-wash. The difference in* coffee processing is used as the basis for changing the type of coffee. Natural is coffee that is dried together with the skin, *honey* is dried without washing, and *full wash* is washed clean before being dried. Based on these three methods, there is a difference in the taste of Palintang coffee. *One of the characteristics of Palintang Coffee is that* it grows naturally and abundantly in the Palintang mountain forest area. Palintang Coffee is sold at a price based on the processing process as follows: Palintang Coffee with the *Fully Wash Dry Hull type* for IDR 300,000 (Three hundred thousand rupiah) per kilogram; *Honey type* for IDR 450,000 (Four hundred thousand rupiah) per kilogram; and the *Natural type* is sold at a price of Rp. 600,000 (six hundred thousand rupiah) per kilogram. It is further known that coffee farmers in Palintang apply the concept of micro lot coffee business concept , a method of coffee production and processing that focuses on the geographical location of the land. The land used tends to be not too large because they believe that the natural conditions around the land will affect the quality and taste of the coffee

Challenges faced by coffee farmers in Balegede Village.
This village has great potential in coffee production, but often UMKM actors face various challenges that hinder the development of their businesses. These challenges include access to technology, product marketing, and limited insight into innovations in coffee processed products. This village has extraordinary coffee potential, but is still faced with various obstacles, ranging from ineffective business management to a lack of understanding of modern coffee processing technology.

The need for technological innovation to increase added value.
The progress of the era is inseparable from the increasingly developing technology. One of the developments in technology is in the agricultural sector. Technology plays a role in increasing the growth of development and efficiency of agricultural productivity. In addition, the application of technology has the potential to create great added value so that people's

purchasing power for agricultural products will increase.

Technological innovation in agriculture can be in the form of using superior seeds, using agricultural machinery, and fertilization. Superior seeds are seeds that have guaranteed quality so that they can guarantee the success of farming efforts. Agricultural tools and machinery can improve the quality and efficiency in cultivating agricultural land. Fertilization is done to provide nutrients to plants to increase production.

Related to that, efforts to maintain and increase agricultural productivity, extension activities and farmer assistance are also keywords. Extension activities, especially from young people, can also be carried out to provide insight to farmers to find out about technological innovations in increasing agricultural productivity.

In addition, the extension also aims to make farmers more competitive in increasing national agricultural productivity. The existence of technological innovation in the agricultural sector is expected to make it easier for farmers to manage agricultural land while increasing the added value of national agricultural commodities.

1.2. Purpose of the Book

The aims of the book are as follows:

1. Inspiring the development of village-based micro-enterprises. This book is intended to be an inspiration for village-based micro-enterprises where these micro-enterprises depend largely on the creativity and innovation of local products that can penetrate national and international markets.
2. Showing the success of technological innovation in coffee processing. Technological innovation in coffee processing in Indonesia, especially in Bandung has shown evidence where Indonesian coffee, especially West Java.
3. Motivating collaboration between academics, government, and MSME actors. Collaboration between Higher Education Institutions and MSME actors is covered by the third Tri Dharma of Higher Education activity, namely Community Service activities.

1.3. Benefits of Books

This book has the benefits of being able to be used as:

a) References for technology-based MSME development.

b) Practical guidance and instructions in relation to the implementation of the mentoring program.

CHAPTER 2. PORTRAIT OF BALEGEDE VILLAGE AND BRINGKA COFFEE

2.1. History of Balegede Village

The origin of the village and its natural potential.

Balegede is a village in Naringgul District , Cianjur , West Java , Indonesia . Which is the most corner village and is the border between Cianjur and Bandung . Administratively, Balegede Village is one of eleven villages in Naringgul District located in the south of Cianjur with a distance to the district capital of 168 km. While the distance from the capital of Bandung Regency is 20 km. Balegede Village has an altitude of 700 meters above sea level. This village is also the entrance to Cianjur Regency to Jayanti Beach.

The history of Balegede Village cannot be separated from one of the figures who was one of the founders of Balegede, namely Eyang Rangga Sadane/Eyang Jaga Niti, who was the twin brother of Eyang Rangga Sadana, the founder of Kadu Agung Village/Ciwidey Village now. They traveled to spread Islam using the southern route, from Ujunggenteng, Sindangbarang and Cidaun. Then they arrived in the wilderness which later became Balegede Village. So it was decided that the one who took care of the village was Eyang Rangga Sadane. While Eyang Rangga Sadana continued his journey until he arrived in Kadu Agung/Ciwidey.

The 41st anniversary of Dalegede Village. Which falls on October 14, 2018, coincides with the date 03-02-Year 1440 H. We need to take a moment to look at the history of the genealogy of Balegede Village and Balegede Village, which is now in the 3rd century.

In the mid-18th century Balegede, Balegede has formed a village that is already known throughout West Java. at that time led by the descendants of the first and second Embah during the Dutch colonial era, the livelihood of the residents at that time was farming or cultivating and began to make new rice field printing called Sawah Lega, now the water channel is from the Citarengtong river and the rice field printing is from the northern part, namely at the Batu Cupu location, now and expanded at the end of the 18th century to the beginning of the 19th century.

Population growth in the early 19th century was increasingly rapid, educational development was also increasingly advanced, education at that time was a three-year elementary school plus BAHP Illiteracy Education to keep up with the progress of the times. In religious education at that time it was led by a Kiyai named Kiyai Nursi as (Lebe) and in 1998 a 6-year elementary school was established which was located in the village of Pasar SDN Balegede now. At that time it was led by the descendants of the 3rd Embah and the fourth descendants and the formation of Kampung Balegede became a Kepunduhan or Kedusunan now which includes several RT and RW. Balegede's status increased in the mid-14th century at the beginning of the Japanese occupation, the geographical location and monographic population of Balegede became more organized, the community's lifestyle also improved, both in terms of education, economics, social and culture.

In 1950, sports became more advanced, Balegede Market was established at the end of the Second Dutch colonial period.

Balegede's status is increasing, which was originally the Balegede sub-district of Naringgul. In 1977, Balegede Village, Naringgul District, was established, whose village head/lurahn was led by Mr. Abas Soleh from Naringgul.

In 1987 Balegede Village participated in the Cianjur Regency Swakarya Village competition, led by Mr. Aprin, the village head. Alhamdulillah Balegede Village was able to win the title of Champion II Swakarya Village in Cianjur Regency and SD N Balegede also has the title of SD Center.

With the following limits:
· North = Bandung Regency
· West = Cikadu District
· East = Sukabakti Village
· South = Wanasari Village

Miduana Traditional Village not only has the potential for natural tourism, but can also be used as one of the cultural education tourism destinations, this is because the character of the local community still holds noble values that can be used as an educational medium for visitors who come. Visitors or tourists who come to Miduana Traditional Village are not only presented with natural beauty, but will also receive an explanation regarding the tourism potential and noble values held by the local community.

Tourism Potential of Miduana Traditional Village Miduana Traditional Village has the potential for cultural educational tourism, some of which are:

1) Architecture of Community Housing
2) Cipandak River, as well as
3) Batu Rompe Site.

The architecture of the community's houses is used as a cultural educational tour because the community's houses have a philosophy that can be used as a medium for educating visitors. The Cipandak River is a river located in the Miduana Traditional Village, which is the place where the Mandi Kahirupan /Cikahirupan/Cai Kahirupan tradition is carried out, namely the tradition of bathing or cleansing oneself before entering the month of Ramadan which is followed by the entire community of the Miduana Traditional Village.

The next potential owned by the Miduana Traditional Village is the Batu Rompe Site which is believed by the local community to be a remnant of thousands of years ago in the form of broken stones that are thought to have been destroyed by a disaster. Uniquely, the stones at the Batu Rompe Site can produce tones.

The role of coffee in the lives of the Balegede community.

Coffee is one of the plantation products that has a fairly high economic value among other plantation crops and plays a role as a necessity for the community in Balegede Village, coffee plants also require support from all parties, and most coffee plantations apply cultivation technology that is still limited so that the coffee plantations are improved so that the plantation business can be successful, so that production results can be increased and can meet the income standards of the plantation owners so that they can improve the welfare of their families.

Most people prefer to plant coffee compared to planting rice because it is caused by the structure of the soil which has a tropical climate so that later the coffee plants that have been planted will grow well according to the temperature, the soil with good texture or structure is soil that comes from volcanic ash or which contains enough sand, so that the circulation of air and water in the soil runs well. The development of coffee is currently quite good because it is seen from the results and coffee plants also have a very important role in economic growth .

In free trade, coffee commodities as the main raw material for the ground coffee industry, and become a determinant of competitiveness in the export market and not only in the form of beans, but in the form of processed coffee, such as ground coffee, and dissolved coffee so that it can be enjoyed by coffee processing farmers. With good and appropriate cultivation techniques, good production quality (coffee beans) is produced and in accordance with consumer desires. The plantation sector is a sector that plays a role as a foreign exchange earner for the country, one of the foreign exchange earning plantation commodities. This role can be in the form of opening up job opportunities, as well as a source of income for farmers, the management of coffee commodities has opened up opportunities for five million farmers. The production of the authenticity of the quality of the coffee beans can be proven through examination and the existence of a certificate of authenticity from the origin of the quality of the coffee beans, thus each consumer can trace the origin of the authenticity of the coffee beans, and coffee beans are usually sold in very limited quantities so that marketing is carried out to various countries because these coffee beans are very popular with various countries so that marketing is very limited starting from the packaging that is made to those that have not been packaged, then it is made well and safely, or to special.

2.2. Bringka Coffee: Characteristics and Potential

A superior type of coffee from Balegede.

Coffee produced by Balegede Village is marketed in the form of coffee fruit, green coffee beans, coffee beans and coffee grounds. Coffee in Indonesia has an important role as a source of foreign exchange because it has a high economic value. One of the areas in Indonesia as a producer of Robusta coffee is Cianjur Regency. Balegede Village, Naringgul District is one part of Cianjur Regency which produces coffee as a superior commodity. In addition to Robusta coffee, there is Arabica Balegede coffee which is quite well-known in several E-Commerce.

Robusta coffee represents between 40% and 45% of global coffee production, with the remainder being *Coffea arabica* . There are some differences in the composition of coffee beans from *C. arabica* and *C. robusta* . *C. robusta* beans tend to have lower acidity, more bitterness, and a woodier, less fruity flavor than *C. arabica beans* .

The traditional process of processing Bringka coffee.

1. Natural Process

This natural process is also known as *the dry process.* This process is one of the oldest techniques in the history of coffee processing. After being harvested, the coffee cherries will be spread on plastic mats and dried in the sun. Some coffee producers sometimes dry them on brick terraces or on special drying tables that have *airflow* at the bottom. When dried in the sun, these coffee beans must be turned over periodically so that the coffee beans dry evenly, and to avoid mold/rot.

In the natural process, the dried coffee fruit is still in the form of fruit/cherry, complete with all its layers. This natural and organic process will make the cherry fermented naturally because the outer skin of the cherry will peel off by itself.

1. Washed Process

The coffee processing process is known as the *wet process.* Generally, this process aims to remove all the fleshy skins attached to the coffee beans before drying. After being harvested, the coffee cherries are usually 'selected' first by soaking them in water. The floating cherries will be discarded, while the sinking ones will be left for further processing because such cherries are considered ripe.

Next, the outer skin and the flesh of the coffee cherry will be removed using a special machine called a depulper . *The* coffee beans that have been removed from their skin are then cleaned again by putting them in a special vessel filled with water so that the remaining skin that is still attached can be completely removed due to the fermentation process.

2.3. Challenges and Opportunities

Problems in the local coffee supply chain.

In this increasingly modern era, opportunities and challenges in the business world are increasing. What needs to be seen in improving the quality and business development of coffee commodities is how to manage their management, especially in supply chain management. The importance of Supply Chain Management in the business world is very necessary to support the success of a business, so that later it will bring great benefits, especially for business development and the provision of quality coffee commodities. The most common problem for farmers is limited market information so that farmers do not know who the product will be sold to with the best profit.

Problems faced by chain actors include (1) limited market control, products produced are not yet oriented towards quality, packaging, labeling, branding, composition, expiration date, and product benefits have not been considered, promotion has not been carried out, and product distribution is still on a local scale, (2) processing technology still relies on assistance from machines and production equipment from the Regency or Provincial Government, and has not been utilized optimally, (3) limited access to capital or financing causes agricultural product processing businesses to not run smoothly (Fitriani et al., 2019). Very low price fluctuations and uncertainty on the sales side are seasonal phenomena that often harm coffee farmers. Farmers' access to information on coffee selling prices at various levels of trade institutions is very limited.

The difference in selling price is often not immediately known by farmers. Village collectors of robusta coffee are generally located far from the coffee plantations. As a result, the transportation costs incurred by village collectors and wholesalers further depress the selling price received by farmers to be lower. The severely damaged road infrastructure that must be taken to distribute coffee from the coffee plantation areas of farmers causes the intensity of shipments to decrease (requiring a relatively longer time for each shipment) and increases transportation costs. This also depresses coffee prices at the farmer level (Fitriani et al., 2011). The problems faced by supply chain actors (suppliers, producers and retailers) are centered on the availability of raw materials which at certain times experience scarcity. This scarcity of raw materials causes price spikes and delays in the production and distribution process (Leppe et al., 2019).

Export opportunities and introduction to global markets.

Indonesian coffee actually has great potential to be exported by SMEs in Indonesia. However, the current performance of Indonesian coffee exports does not reflect this. There has been a decline in performance in coffee exports, especially in 2018.

Although Indonesia is the fourth largest producer in the world, in terms of exports it only ranked 13th in 2018, a sharp decline from its previous rank of 7th in 2017. The world coffee trade is still dominated by Brazil with a world market share of around 14.3% with a value of 4.3 billion USD. Then the second rank is always occupied by Vietnam with a market share of around 9.4%. Other coffee producing countries that beat Indonesia's exports are

Colombia, Honduras, and Ethiopia. In fact, several countries that are not coffee producers can beat Indonesia's exports, such as Germany, Switzerland, Italy, the United States, the Netherlands, etc. This is because these developed countries control the coffee *roasting industry* and other coffee processing.

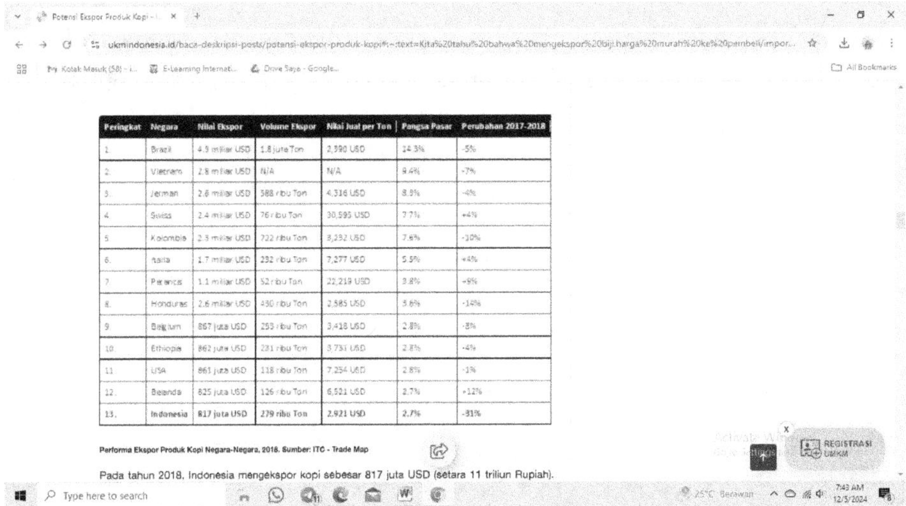

Peringkat	Negara	Nilai Ekspor	Volume Ekspor	Nilai Jual per Ton	Pangsa Pasar	Perubahan 2017-2018
1.	Brazil	4.3 miliar USD	1.8 juta Ton	2,390 USD	14.3%	-5%
2.	Vietnam	2.8 miliar USD	N/A	N/A	9.4%	-7%
3.	Jerman	2.6 miliar USD	588 ribu Ton	4,316 USD	8.9%	-4%
4.	Swiss	2.4 miliar USD	76 ribu Ton	30,595 USD	7.7%	+4%
5.	Kolombia	2.3 miliar USD	722 ribu Ton	3,232 USD	7.6%	-10%
6.	Italia	1.7 miliar USD	232 ribu Ton	7,277 USD	5.5%	+4%
7.	Perancis	1.1 miliar USD	52 ribu Ton	22,219 USD	3.8%	+9%
8.	Honduras	2.6 miliar USD	430 ribu Ton	2,585 USD	5.6%	-14%
9.	Belgium	867 juta USD	253 ribu Ton	3,418 USD	2.8%	-3%
10.	Ethiopia	862 juta USD	231 ribu Ton	3,731 USD	2.8%	-4%
11.	USA	861 juta USD	118 ribu Ton	7,254 USD	2.8%	-1%
12.	Belanda	825 juta USD	126 ribu Ton	6,521 USD	2.7%	+12%
13.	Indonesia	817 juta USD	279 ribu Ton	2,921 USD	2.7%	-31%

Performa Ekspor Produk Kopi Negara-Negara, 2018. Sumber: ITC - Trade Map

Pada tahun 2018, Indonesia mengekspor kopi sebesar 817 juta USD (setara 11 triliun Rupiah).

In 2018, Indonesia exported coffee worth 817 million USD (equivalent to 11 trillion Rupiah). This value decreased compared to the value in 2014-2017 which was always above 1 billion USD. There was even a decrease of 31% in 2017. One of the factors is domestic coffee consumption which always increases by 8 percent from year to year. The most unfortunate thing is the low selling value of Indonesian coffee products which is only 2,921 USD per Ton, most of which are cheap raw coffee beans. This indicates that Indonesian coffee must be exported with a production process that produces much higher added value.

In the case of coffee, there is an increasing trend towards the fifth phase of global coffee consumption, where coffee consumers will focus more on the concept of high-quality artisan coffee produced on a small scale but with a *sustainable process* and adequate technology. However, market conditions in Indonesia are still in the second phase, where they are still focused on well-known coffee cafe brands, such as Starbucks. Even now, there are many popular coffee cafe brands from Indonesia, such as Kopi Kenangan, Janji Jiwa, and others. This indicates that with domestic coffee consumption continuing to increase, market-class coffee no longer needs to be exported. To answer the trend in the global coffee market to successfully export Indonesian coffee, the answer is none other than to focus on *specialty* and *sustainable coffee. Especially for businesses at the SME level that are unable to export in large volumes, playing exports on specialty* and *sustainable* coffee in small volumes is the best solution.

Chapter 3. Technology and Innovation in Bringka Coffee Processing

3.1. Introduction to Technology in Coffee Farming and Processing
Modern processing tools and machines.

1. Scales

Scales are tools used to measure the weight of coffee raw materials that will be used so that the bean processing process can be processed properly. How it works, Coffee beans are placed in a container then use the main scale and the smallest unit to weigh the weight of the coffee.

1. Pulper Machine

The pulper machine is a tool used to peel the skin of fresh, red coffee beans that have just been harvested. How it works, The coffee bean skin is rubbed by a rotating cylinder (rotor) on the surface of a stationary plate (stator). The coffee beans are inserted through a funnel and fall on the surface of the rotor. The coffee beans that pass through the first cylinder will be peeled in the second cylinder. The rotational force of the cylinder pushes the coffee beans until they are squeezed and crushed on the surface of the stator so that the skin of the fruit is peeled off the coffee beans. Water is sprayed into the peeling gap to help the peeling mechanism, cleaning, and reducing the shear force of the cylinder so that the horn skin does not break.

1. Dryer House

The drying room is a place where coffee is in the drying process using sunlight. The walls of the room are made of plastic so that the coffee is not exposed to direct sunlight, dust, smoke, rain and other environmental factors. In addition, it can also stabilize the room temperature. How it works, Drying station or drying house is made in such a way that the sun can absorb more from various sides and the coffee will dry faster.

1. Huller Machine

Coffee Huller Machine is a machine used to peel previously dried coffee and separate clean coffee beans from their horn skin. How it works, Coffee fruit that is inserted through the hopper at the top of the machine is processed using a knife attached to a rotating shaft or roller at a speed in rpm according to specifications, dimensions and rotational power in horse power.

1. Grader Machine

Grader Machine is a machine that functions to determine the size of coffee beans according to the size of the beans, in addition to grouping the size of this machine will separate non-coffee bean impurities. How it works, Dry coffee beans are put on the sieve, then with a vibration system, the coffee will be sorted according to the desired size. Coffee beans will be separated according to size and will come out through the existing channel.

1. Roaster Machine

A roaster machine is a machine used to help cook coffee beans in a measured and controlled manner. How it works, Heating coffee beans with the help of a heating machine until the color or ripening of the coffee beans is formed. Namely there are 3 stages, namely light, medium and dark.

1. Grinding Machine

A grinding machine is a machine used to grind roasted coffee beans into powder. How it works, Roasted coffee beans are put into the machine then the rotor rotates so that coffee powder can be formed.

1. Sealer

The sealer machine is a machine used to assist in the packaging process of a product that has a plastic wrap. How it works, By inducing heat from the filament to the Teflon layer which is eventually channeled to the plastic layer. This causes the heat from the filament to be absorbed by the plastic so that the plastic packaging sticks.

IT-based coffee processing technology.

Digital marketing is one of the important aspects in the development of micro, small, and medium enterprises (MSMEs), especially for coffee entrepreneurs in Balegede Village. In the 'Kopi Bringka' mentoring activity, IT-based digital marketing training is provided to help MSMEs utilize technology to reach a wider market. This training covers a variety of materials, from a basic introduction to digital marketing to advanced techniques to increase product visibility.

One of the techniques emphasized in this training is the use of social media. Platforms such as Instagram and Facebook are efficient tools for promoting coffee products. Participants are taught how to create interesting content that can attract the attention of potential consumers. The use of quality images, compelling captions, and the use of relevant hashtags can increase audience interaction and reach. In addition, the training also includes strategies for building a loyal online community, which can play an important role in promoting products organically.

In addition to social media, there is also an introduction to the e-commerce platform. In today's digital era, e-commerce has become an important channel for MSMEs to sell products directly to consumers without geographical limitations. Through this platform, participants are taught how to register, create an online store, and manage inventory. The key to success in selling through e-commerce is understanding SEO (Search Engine Optimization) strategies and using paid advertising to attract more buyers. By optimizing digital marketing, coffee MSMEs in Balegede Village can not only increase sales, but also increase customer brand awareness in the wider market.

One of the final processes to get good coffee beans is through the roasting process. The working principle of a manual roasting machine is to heat the coffee in a rotating oven at a certain temperature to distribute heat evenly. One type of coffee oven heater is an electric heating element, where the working system is still controlled manually with a switch or controlled semi-automatically using a timer operated by the operator.

Internet Of Things (IOT) is anything or electronic devices that can interact directly with users that are used for monitoring or control needs on the device via the internet. Therefore, by utilizing Internet of Things-based technology, it can facilitate the control of the roasting process, namely by setting and adjusting the temperature and time levels through microcontroller devices and monitoring devices such as sensors that can be controlled directly through microcontrollers.

One of the technologies that can be used is embedded system technology. An embedded system is a computer system embedded in a particular device or system, which is able to perform various functions and tasks automatically with simple input and output. By using embedded system technology, coffee bean drying can be done automatically and more effectively, so that it can speed up the drying process of coffee beans. This system is a prototype as an illustration for a coffee bean dryer. This tool has a roof cover that will be closed to protect the coffee beans from rainfall and will open when the weather is sunny. In addition, this tool has a heater in the form of an incandescent lamp that will help the drying process at night at 17.00 until morning at 07.00, and when it rains.

3.2. Bringka Coffee Product Innovation

Coffee-based food creations (examples: coffee candy, coffee cake).

Kopi Bringka provides space for entrepreneurs in Balegede Village to innovate in producing various interesting and quality coffee preparations. By relying on local coffee raw materials, entrepreneurs are not only able to produce coffee in the form of traditional drinks, but also develop other creative products that have wide market potential. One of the popular innovations is serving coffee with a distinctive, appetizing taste. Entrepreneurs utilize various natural ingredients, such as spices and fruits, to create unique and attractive flavor combinations for consumers.

In addition, coffee-based snacks have also become a highlight. Various types of snacks, such as biscuits, brownies, and other light cakes, inspired by the taste of coffee provide an alternative for coffee lovers. This innovation not only expands the reach of the product, but also provides added value to local coffee, making it a versatile raw material. With the presence of coffee-based snacks, many consumers have found a new experience in enjoying coffee, both as a drink and as food.

In addition to consumer products, innovation in the beauty industry is also worth noting. Several business actors have succeeded in creating coffee-based skincare products. The antioxidant content in coffee is believed to provide benefits for the skin, from maintaining moisture to helping the cell regeneration process. The use of coffee in beauty products shows that the potential of local coffee is not only limited to the culinary sector, but also reaches the health and beauty industry. Thus, the development of innovative coffee processing is a great opportunity for MSMEs in Balegede Village to achieve success, as well as introduce Bringka coffee to the wider community.

Development of instant coffee and cold brew variants.

Cold brew coffee is a method of coffee extraction that does not require heat. The cold brew extraction process requires a temperature of $20\,^{\circ}$ -$25\,^{\circ}$ C or lower with a time of 8-24 hours. The advantages of cold brew coffee with hot brewed coffee are that cold brew coffee has low acid and bitter characteristics, and is a practical coffee product made from original coffee.

Cold Brew is a method of brewing coffee by soaking coarsely ground coffee powder in room temperature water for 12-24 hours and then serving it with ice cubes as a cold coffee drink.

Cold brew coffee is the most popular because of its smooth taste and almost unlike coffee, some coffee shops choose *cold brew coffee* as their signature recipe. Some baristas even add a little coffee syrup to give a more special taste impression. If you want to find out which *cold brew coffee ratio* is best for your coffee drinking activity, I suggest making it yourself at home.

Based on the ratio of coffee and water when making cold brew coffee, the ratio of 1:6 - 1:8 the less water tends to produce a strong coffee character also called concentrated coffee, and 1:15 - 1:18 will give a soft *cold brew coffee character. The character of cold brew coffee* is served with ice cubes because when the ice cubes slowly melt, it makes it more impressive to present a soft sweet taste.

To make *cold brew coffee* is fairly easy, just know the concept of the ratio of coffee used and use a coarse grind. Interestingly, making *cold brew coffee* can also be done without using a *cold brewer coffee tool* , however, of course the resulting character will be different. *Cold brew* without *a cold brewer* generally uses a jarless or similar container, when it has reached the desired brewing duration then filtered with filter paper or a cloth filter.

Definition of Cold Brew

Cold brew is a method of preparing coffee using cold water to extract the flavor and aroma of the coffee over several hours. This method is different from traditional coffee brewing which uses hot water to extract the coffee flavor instantly.

Stages in Using the Cold Brew Technique

After understanding the meaning of the *cold brew technique* , here are some steps for brewing coffee using the *cold brew technique* :

1. Preparing Coffee Beans

Choose good quality coffee beans and grind them first, so they are suitable for brewing with cold water.

2. Mix Coffee Powder with Cold Water

Put the ground coffee in a container and add cold water. The ratio of ground coffee to water is usually 1:4 or 1:5. Stir well until the coffee is submerged in water.

3. Soak Coffee Grounds in Cold Water

Cover the container and store in a cool place for at least 12 hours or more depending on personal preference. The longer it steeps, the stronger the coffee flavor.

4. Filter the Coffee

After the brewing process is complete, strain the coffee from the water using a strainer or coffee cloth. A filter can be used to separate the coffee grounds from the water, while a coffee cloth is usually used to strain the coffee so that the *cold brew results* are clearer.

5. Enjoy Coffee

Cold brew coffee can be served in a glass with ice cubes and milk if desired. This cold brew coffee can be stored in the refrigerator for several days.

Cold brew is an easy and convenient way to make coffee and can be an alternative for coffee lovers who want a smoother *and* less bitter taste.

3.3. Digital Transformation in Marketing

Utilization of e-commerce: Bringka Techno Platform.

In the digital era, market access is an important factor that can increase the success of MSMEs, including in the coffee processing product sector. Bringka Coffee was introduced to several digital platforms designed to help them reach a wider market. By utilizing technology, MSMEs in Balegede Village can introduce and market their coffee products not only locally but also in the national market.

E-commerce platforms such as Tokopedia and Bukalapak have become the favorite choice for many small business owners to sell their products online. Through these platforms, MSMEs can easily organize product displays, receive orders, and make transactions more efficiently. This not only increases the visibility of their coffee products but also provides an opportunity to interact directly with consumers. Feedback obtained from consumers can also be used to improve the quality and types of products offered.

In addition, social media such as Instagram and Facebook are also effective means of marketing coffee products. By utilizing attractive visual content, MSMEs can promote their uniqueness, such as traditional coffee processing, flavor variants, and the story behind the product. This approach not only targets local buyers, but can also attract the interest of consumers outside the wider region through the right marketing strategy.

With access to the digital platform, it is expected that sales of coffee products from Balegede Village can increase significantly. MSMEs who previously only relied on local sales now have the opportunity to reach a wider market, and adapt to changing consumer trends and demands.

Digital branding and marketing strategies.

The importance of branding and product packaging cannot be ignored in the world of micro, small, and medium enterprises (MSMEs), especially in Balegede Village which relies on coffee as its main commodity. Strong branding creates a positive image in the minds of consumers, which can increase trust and preference for the coffee products produced. In this context, visual identity is one of the key elements that needs to be considered. Visual identity includes logos, colors, and typography used in every aspect of brand communication. With a consistent and attractive design, processed coffee products from MSMEs can be more easily recognized in an increasingly competitive market.

Packaging design also plays an important role in attracting consumers. Attractive packaging will not only make the product look more professional, but can also create the impression that the product is of high quality. In the 'Kopi Bringka' mentoring activity, participants were invited to design packaging that was not only aesthetic but also functional. This pilot project prioritizes the use of environmentally friendly materials and ergonomic design, making it easier for consumers to use and store coffee products.

Through a combination of strong branding and effective packaging, UMKM actors in Balegede Village can increase the competitiveness of their products. Consumers today pay close attention not only to product quality, but also to the message conveyed through branding and packaging. Therefore, investing in developing a good visual identity and packaging design is a strategic step that can attract more customers. This is expected to have a positive impact on the growth of UMKM, so that processed coffee products can penetrate a wider market.

After creating strong branding and effective packaging, MSMEs can start marketing their coffee products on e-commerce platforms such as Tokopedia and Bukalapak, which have become favorite choices for many small business owners to sell their products online. In addition, social media such as Instagram and Facebook are also effective means of marketing coffee products. By utilizing attractive visual content, MSMEs can promote their uniqueness, such as traditional coffee processing, flavor variants, and the story behind the product. This approach not only targets local buyers but can also attract consumers outside the wider region through the right marketing strategy.

CHAPTER 4. MENTORING AND COLLABORATION PROCESS

4.1. Stages of Bringka Coffee MSME Mentoring

Planning and analysis of MSME needs.

1. MSME Performance

MSME performance is the extent to which MSMEs achieve financial and non-financial goals (Pulka, 2021). Through qualitative and quantitative perspectives, MSME performance can be understood (Cicea et al., 2019). MSME performance is seen as the company's ability to achieve sales and profitability targets, as well as a non-financial perspective on competitors (Wilden et al., 2013). Likewise, for Vij and Bedi (2016), MSME performance is an overall index of MSMEs' ability to satisfy their stakeholders, measured by financial and non-financial indicators; while the assessment indicators for Santos and Brito (2014) include profitability, market value, growth, social performance, environmental performance, employee satisfaction, and customer satisfaction.

1. Capital Accessibility/Ease of Access to Capital

The main problem of Indonesian MSMEs is capital with a percentage of 51.09% (Kemenkop-UKM, 2020). Based on these capital problems and aligned with the framework proposed by Chen et al. (2016), valence capital accessibility at the physiological needs level in Maslow's hierarchy because finance is an important element in determining the growth and survival of MSMEs. In addition, finance is the oxygen and lifeblood of every organization (Malepati et al., 2022; Sharan, 1967). Access to finance helps small businesses to invest and contribute to national economic development and poverty alleviation (Osano and Languitone, 2015). The results of the study showed a positive relationship between access to finance and company performance (World Bank, 2013; Bongomin et al., 2017).

1. **Information Technology**

Information Technology (IT) is an important support for the development of MSMEs today. IT greatly helps MSMEs to align business strategies and achieve business goals (Chen and Tsou, 2007). The number of MSMEs that have been digitalized is still relatively small, around 12 million MSMEs or only reaching 19% (Kemenkop-UKM, 2021). Based on these IT problems and aligned with the framework proposed by Chen et al. (2016), valencing IT at the level of security needs in Maslow's hierarchy because information technology can increase the sense of security for the sustainability of MSMEs. The sense of security of MSMEs in this digital era can increase if MSMEs implement the required technology because IT adoption helps MSMEs to achieve operational performance and remain competitive in the global market (Tripathy et al., 2016). In addition, IT adoption can increase productivity and efficiency in all MSME activities (Kim et al., 2020). Research results show a positive relationship between information technology and firm performance (Borah et al., 2022; Chege and Wang, 2020; Tripathy et al., 2016; Huang et al., 2022).

1. **Quality of Service**

The results of a survey by the Ministry of Cooperatives and SMEs together with the Indonesian E-Commerce Association showed that 75% of MSMEs that have entered e-commerce have difficulty meeting aspects of quality, consistency of the same product and maintaining after-sales service. The products provided by MSMEs do not yet have clear standards (Kemenkop-UKM, 2021). Based on these service quality problems and aligned with the framework proposed by Chen et al. (2016), valences service quality at the level of love, affection, and belonging needs in Maslow's hierarchy, because service quality refers to social relationships with colleagues and customers. MSMEs seem to want to create a romantic relationship between their brands and consumers, while continuing to build their business (Stoll and Ha-Brookshire, 2012). This relationship is considered important for creating and maintaining consumer loyalty (Stoll and Ha-Brookshire, 2012). Consumer loyalty will be established because consumers believe in the quality of the service provided and are able to reduce the risks obtained (Hess and John, 2005). Service quality and customer satisfaction are closely related and influence each other (Sureshchandar et al., 2002). By improving service quality and customer satisfaction, organizational performance can increase (Sumardi and Fernandes, 2020). The results of the study showed a positive relationship between service quality and performance (Amos et al., 2021).

1. **Competitive Advantage**

The government has a mission through the implementation of the 2020-2024 RPJMN (National Medium-Term Development Plan) policy which strongly supports MSMEs to be able to compete in both domestic and global markets with a strategy of increasing the competitive advantage of each MSME via various factors (Kemenkop-UKM, 2020). Based on the importance of the competitive advantage of each MSME and aligned with the framework proposed by Chen et al. (2016), valences competitive advantage at the level of appreciation or recognition needs in Maslow's hierarchy. MSMEs that are able to meet the need for competitive advantage are able to gain recognition and appreciation in their market. Competitive advantage refers to the superiority of comparative position in the market that leads companies to surpass their competitors (Zhou et al., 2009). It is very important to achieve and maintain competitive advantage as a strategic step for superior company performance (Kaleka and Morgan, 2017). The results of the study showed a positive relationship between service quality and performance (Kaleka and Morgan, 2017; Zhou et al., 2009).

1. **Innovation**

The small number of MSME products that penetrate the international market is due to the low level of creativity possessed by MSME actors and low product innovation (Kemenkop-UKM, 2020). Based on these innovation problems and aligned with the framework proposed by Chen et al. (2016), the authors valence innovation at the level of self-actualization needs in Maslow's hierarchy. Innovation is a condition that is considered new in the form of ideas or goods and services (Kotler and Keller, 2012). Innovation carried out by MSMEs is a form of developing self-potential to meet the highest needs of the MSME itself. Innovation is the key to organizational survival because innovation can facilitate companies to succeed in an increasingly dynamic and competitive market (Hogan and Coote, 2014). Innovative performance has a positive impact on the company both in the long and short term. If innovative performance increases, production and marketing performance can improve, and result in a gradual increase in financial performance (Gunday et al., 2011).

Application of technology in production and distribution.

The role of information technology in the logistics business greatly assists the planning, implementation and supervision of the process of moving goods from one place to another.

This includes assistance during packing, storage in the warehouse, and distribution of goods to the market. With today's developing information technology, the logistics process is faster, more accurate, and more efficient.

Examples of Information Technology in Logistics Business

Nowadays, there are several software used in the logistics world. The most famous is WMS. Besides that, there are several more:

- WMS (Warehouse Management System)
- CRM (Customer Relationship Management)
- EDI (Electronic Data Interchange)
- ERP (Enterprise Resource Planning)
- TMS (Transportation Management System)

But let's take a look at the (popular) technology trends that have made their way into the world of logistics in recent years.

1. Warehouse Management System (WMS): technology that greatly assists operational activities in the warehouse. Its tasks include: monitoring incoming and outgoing goods, viewing stock, conditions, and inventory activities are made easier with WMS.
2. Blockchain: usually used for finance, because it works like a digital ledger. With blockchain, the transaction process becomes easier, safer and more transparent. Not only used for finance, in logistics, blockchain is also often relied on for data entry, tracing and tracking.
3. Augmented Reality and Virtual Reality: usually in the gaming world, but for logistics, it can also be, for example, the logistics company owned by DHL. With the concept of combining the virtual and real worlds, thanks to this technology, all DHL employees can easily carry out warehousing activities such as picking up goods, appointing the fastest route, to the process of sending goods.
4. Transport Management System (TMS): its role is very important in the distribution of goods, this technology facilitates the planning, optimization and implementation of transportation operational activities.
5. Drone: This is the latest technology that is used as a tool to send goods. It is used as transportation and to send important packages to someone. Examples of companies that have implemented this technology are Amazon, Wing, and Walgreen.

The application of the above technology has not been fully followed by Indonesia. But as time goes by, we will take part in the future. In addition, if we look at the use of technology in the logistics sector in Indonesia, the most obvious is the use of the internet and applications, such as Gojek which presents the Go Box feature, a goods transport service. Or logistics applications from other companies such as Deliveree, Kargo.id, Caritruck and others.

The Role of Information Technology in Logistics

Businesses have been digitizing themselves in this decade. One of them is the logistics business. Rather than a choice, it is more of a necessity. Because the presence of technology makes it easier.

And talking about the role of information technology or IT in the logistics sector, you can find the answer below:

1. To speed up business processes and prevent bottlenecks in the demand for goods
2. Companies achieve target times faster, inventory processes are shorter, and efficiency is better. Especially in the manufacturing sector.
3. With IT, companies can more easily meet consumer needs day by day and every day. The most important role of IT is this: managing the supply chain.
4. IT improves the efficiency of data exchange, such as shipping verification data, order processing, billing and shipping advice.
5. Able to track the physical location of each order. This activity would not be possible without the use of technology that currently exists.
6. Improving access to information by providing quality information
7. Using information technology in the logistics business can also reduce costs.

Evaluation of the success of the mentoring program.

The 'Kopi Bringka' mentoring activity has had a significant impact on Micro, Small, and Medium Enterprises (MSMEs) in Balegede Village. The training focused on the development of innovative coffee products, utilizing the latest technology to improve product quality and competitiveness. One of the real results of this activity is the emergence of various high-quality coffee products, such as premium ground coffee, sachet coffee, and various ready-to-drink coffee products that are attractive to consumers.

The Balegede Village community not only learned about good coffee processing techniques, but also how to market their products effectively. This training brings new hope to MSMEs, who now have more skills and knowledge in developing coffee-based products. Generally, MSMEs feel more confident in creating product innovations that can be accepted by a wider market. In addition, they can now utilize digital platforms to promote their products, which they had not previously thought of much.

Not only new products are produced, but also marketing and management skills are improved. The hope for the future is that MSMEs can continue to develop and introduce more creative coffee product variants , so that they can meet the diverse tastes of consumers. It is also hoped that there will be further collaboration with related parties, such as local governments and financial institutions, to assist in funding and strengthening product marketing. With these steps, the potential of coffee in Balegede Village can be maximized, and is expected to contribute to the local economy and improve the welfare of the local community.

4.2. Collaboration with Stakeholders

The role of universities, local governments and the private sector.

The development of the Micro, Small, and Medium Enterprises (MSMEs) sector in Indonesia, especially in Balegede Village, is highly dependent on collaboration between various parties. Strong support from the government and the private sector can be a major driver in the success of activities such as 'Kopi Bringka'. The government, both at the central and regional levels, has a strategic role in providing the policies, regulations, and resources needed to develop these coffee-based MSMEs. This includes providing training, access to capital, and marketing facilities that can help local coffee products reach a wider market.

In addition, there is also an important role played by private institutions.

By establishing cooperation, they can provide financial and technical support. Various companies can contribute through their CSR programs, which not only help increase the production capacity of MSMEs, but also offer training to improve product quality. The exchange of information between the government and the private sector is very important in creating an ecosystem that is conducive to the growth of MSMEs, as seen in the 'Kopi Bringka' activity.

Cooperation between the government and the private sector is not only limited to financial support. Joint development strategies involving research and innovation in coffee products can create new opportunities and increase competitiveness. For example, the ability to utilize information technology in product marketing is a crucial aspect. Through technological support, MSMEs can market their coffee products online, reach wider consumers and increase income.

With full support and good collaboration between all parties, the success of MSMEs in Balegede Village will be increasingly assured. This will have a positive impact on the local economy and at the same time preserve coffee commodities that have great potential.

Strategy for building innovation ecosystem in villages.

Developing a knowledge-based village business ecosystem is a strategic step to improve entrepreneurship and the welfare of rural communities. Here are the steps and key elements to consider:

1. Identification of Local Potential:

- Conduct surveys and analysis to identify economic potential and natural resources that can be utilized in the village.
- Identify local expertise and uniqueness that can form the basis for product or service development.

2. Training and Education:

- Provide training and education on entrepreneurship, business management, and information technology.

- Facilitate learning to improve skills needed in the business world.

3. Village Business Incubator:

- Establish village business incubators as development and support centers for local businesses.
- Provide guidance, facilities and resources to local entrepreneurs.

4. Use of Technology and Innovation:

- Invite village communities to adopt the latest technology that suits local needs.
- Encourage innovation in production processes, marketing, and business management.

5. Networking and Partnerships:

- Build networks and partnerships with companies, educational institutions and other organizations.
- Collaborate with stakeholders to increase support and access to markets.

6. Infrastructure Development:

- Ensure that there is basic infrastructure such as roads, electricity and adequate internet access.
- Provide facilities that support the production and distribution of goods or services.

7. Marketing and Promotion:

- Conduct marketing and promotion of village products or services locally and online.
- Use social media and online platforms to increase visibility.

8. Product Development and Branding:

- Encourage the development of new products or services that reflect local uniqueness and culture.
- Build strong branding to increase competitiveness in the market.

9. Social Entrepreneurship:

- Implement business models that have a positive social impact.
- Focus on community development and environmental sustainability.

10. Inclusive Finance:

- Provide access to inclusive financial services such as cooperatives or micro-banks.
- Help village communities understand the benefits and good financial management.

11. Business Risk Management:

- Provide training on risk management and business continuity.
- Provide assistance regarding business risk management.

12. Strengthening Cooperatives and Business Groups:

- Support the formation of cooperatives or business groups at the village level.
- Facilitate collaboration between local business actors.

13. Empowerment of Women and Youth:

- Prioritize women and youth empowerment in entrepreneurship programs.

- Provide specific training and support to help them contribute actively.

14. Continuous Evaluation and Improvement:

- Conduct periodic evaluations of program success and identify areas for improvement.
- Involve the community in the evaluation process to get valuable feedback.

15. Certification and Quality Program:

- Implement a certification program to ensure the quality of village products or services.
- Certification can increase consumer confidence and market competitiveness.

4.3. Strengthening Human Resources (HR) Capacity

Technical and management skills training.

Micro, Small and Medium Enterprises (MSMEs) play a vital role in the global economy, especially in creating jobs and supporting local economic growth. However, many MSMEs face management challenges that can limit their growth potential. Therefore, specialized management training for MSMEs is an important step in strengthening the foundation of their business and improving their performance.

1. Identify MSME Management Needs

Training should begin with identifying the specific needs of the MSME. This includes financial analysis, inventory management, marketing, and operations. By understanding the challenges faced by each MSME, training can be tailored to suit the context of each business.

2. Financial Training and Business Planning

Many MSMEs have difficulty managing their finances. This training can include creating simple financial reports, budget planning, and understanding the basics of finance. This way, MSMEs can make better decisions regarding investments and expenses.

3. Marketing and Branding

Training in digital marketing strategies, brand management, and increasing online visibility can help MSMEs expand their market share. Increasing online presence through social media and e-commerce platforms can open up new opportunities for MSMEs to reach a wider customer base.

4. Stock and Production Management

Efficient and optimal stock management is the key to the success of MSMEs in maintaining product availability and avoiding excess stock. This training can include forecasting techniques, selecting the right vendor, and improving the production process.

5. Leadership and Team Skills

It is important for SME owners to have strong leadership skills and be able to motivate their team. Leadership training can help them manage conflict, build solid teams, and motivate employees to achieve common goals.

6. Technology and Innovation

Introducing MSMEs to the latest technologies and innovative practices can help them stay relevant in the ever-changing market. This training involves understanding digital tools, e-commerce, and innovation strategies to increase competitiveness.

7. Performance Evaluation and Monitoring

Training is not enough at the initial stage; it is important to have a mechanism for evaluating and monitoring performance afterwards. This allows SMEs to assess the impact of the training on their business and make changes if necessary.

By accessing comprehensive management training, MSMEs can overcome challenges, increase competitiveness, and make a positive contribution to the local economy. This training is not only an investment in MSME business development, but also a strategic step to increase economic resilience at the micro and medium levels.

Ongoing assistance for business sustainability.

Strengthening MSMEs in rural areas is like planting a tree. Its roots that are firmly embedded in every corner of the village will support the welfare of the community like the sturdy trunk of a towering tree. Not to forget, mentoring and training programs become fertilizer that fertilizes the ecosystem of village MSMEs, so that they can grow sustainably and make a real contribution to the progress of the local economy. MSMEs are like the backbone of the village economy. Their existence is the pulse of life that drives the wheels of the economy, opens up employment opportunities, and improves people's standard of living. Unfortunately, there are still many village MSMEs that are constrained in developing their potential optimally. They face challenges such as unorganized business management, limited market access, and minimal ability to adapt to developments in the era.

To overcome these challenges, mentoring and training programs are the right solution. This program provides practical guidance and training to village MSMEs to improve their management skills, develop competitive products and services, and expand market access. With intensive and sustainable mentoring, MSMEs are expected to be able to grow more resiliently, adapt to change, and make a greater contribution to the village economy. One of the main focuses of the mentoring program is to improve MSME business management. Business actors will be guided to prepare a comprehensive business plan, manage finances effectively, and implement an efficient operational system. In addition, they will also receive training related to production planning, quality control, and the use of technology to optimize their business performance.

Mentoring and training programs are also designed to ensure the sustainability of village MSME businesses. Business actors will be equipped with knowledge about sustainable business practices, such as proper waste management, energy conservation, and the application of circular economy principles. By adopting these practices, MSMEs can reduce their environmental impact while increasing their competitiveness in the market. One of the benefits of mentoring and training is increasing the knowledge and skills needed to manage a business effectively. Village MSMEs often lack access to educational and training resources , so they do not have a strong foundation in making business decisions. Mentoring and training provide a solution by equipping MSMEs with knowledge about financial management, marketing, and business operations.

In addition, mentoring and training also offer ongoing support. Village MSMEs often have to face various challenges in running a business, such as tight market competition and lack of access to capital. Mentoring programs provide mentors and experts who can help MSMEs overcome these challenges, provide advice, and provide the moral support they need.

Not only that, mentoring and training also help improve the sustainability of village MSMEs. By gaining the right knowledge and skills, MSMEs can develop strong and sustainable business strategies. They can identify market opportunities, manage finances effectively, and build strategic partnerships. Thus, village MSMEs can survive in the long term and contribute positively to the village economy.

CHAPTER 5. SUCCESS AND IMPACT OF MENTORING

5.1. Results of the Mentoring Program

Improving the quality and quantity of production.

The 'Kopi Bringka' mentoring activity has had a significant impact on Micro, Small, and Medium Enterprises (MSMEs) in Balegede Village. The training focused on the development of innovative coffee products, utilizing the latest technology to improve product quality and competitiveness. One of the real results of this activity is the emergence of various high-quality coffee products, such as premium ground coffee, sachet coffee, and various ready-to-drink coffee products that are attractive to consumers.

The Balegede Village community not only learned about good coffee processing techniques, but also how to market their products effectively. This training brings new hope to MSMEs, who now have more skills and knowledge in developing coffee-based products. Generally, MSMEs feel more confident in creating product innovations that can be accepted by a wider market. In addition, they can now utilize digital platforms to promote their products, which they had not previously thought of much.

Not only new products are produced, but also marketing and management skills are improved. The hope for the future is that MSMEs can continue to develop and introduce more creative coffee product variants, so that they can meet the diverse tastes of consumers. It is also hoped that there will be further collaboration with related parties, such as local governments and financial institutions, to assist in funding and strengthening product marketing. With these steps, the potential of coffee in Balegede Village can be maximized, and is expected to contribute to the local economy and improve the welfare of the local community.

Market expansion through digitalization.

In the ever-growing digital era, marketing through social media and e-commerce plays an important role in business strategy, especially for Micro, Small and Medium Enterprises (MSMEs). For business actors in Balegede Village, the implementation of digital marketing can be the key to increasing the visibility and competitiveness of local coffee products such as Kopi Bringka. The training provided to participants not only focuses on the accumulation of knowledge, but also on real practices that can be applied directly.

Data-driven marketing is the foundation for entrepreneurs in understanding market trends and consumer behavior. By analyzing relevant data, MSMEs can identify the most potential market segments. In addition, an interesting content strategy is a crucial aspect to reach a wider audience. The training includes creating informative and interesting promotional content, so that coffee products can be more easily recognized and remembered by the wider community.

Social media, as an effective marketing platform, allows business people to interact directly with consumers. Managing social media accounts well not only increases engagement but also helps in creating a loyal community. In this case, a personal and authentic approach will make the brand more relatable to consumers. Therefore, participants are trained to manage social media with the right strategy, including storytelling techniques that can trigger consumer interest and emotions.

By increasing competence in the field of digital marketing, MSMEs in Balegede Village are expected to not only be able to survive, but also develop and compete in an increasingly tight market. The implementation of this understanding will open up new opportunities for Kopi Bringka and other local products, making a significant contribution to regional economic growth.

5.2. Social and Economic Impacts in Balegede Village

Increasing local community income.

Unemployment is an acute problem in Indonesia. To overcome this problem, the government is trying to maximize the MSME sector in absorbing a lot of workers because it has been proven that this sector can absorb up to 70%. In addition to MSMEs in urban areas, MSMEs in rural areas also have a fairly high contribution to the economy. This is because most areas in Indonesia are still rural. Job opportunities in villages are not as complex as job opportunities in cities, therefore increasing MSMEs in rural areas is very important to support the economy of rural residents, especially since villages are currently the center of national development in an effort to achieve equitable distribution and acceleration. This is where the important role of the existence of MSMEs is that they are able to drive the economy of the surrounding community and revive other supporting local businesses. The presence of MSME centers is one solution that can resolve the inequality between villages and cities and drive the regional economy in general.

With the presence of assistance for MSMEs and processed coffee products in Balagede village, the local community has been greatly helped, especially with the presence of Bringka Coffee products, which have given the community jobs and increased the income of the local community.

The role of villages in promoting local coffee at national and global levels.

Balegede Village, located in Naringgul District, Cianjur Regency, is undergoing significant changes through an initiative known as 'Kopi Bringka'. This program aims to empower Micro, Small, and Medium Enterprises (MSMEs) in the local coffee sector by integrating the creativity of the local community and digital technology. This transformation not only provides new enthusiasm for coffee entrepreneurs, but also creates wider economic opportunities for the entire community.

With the existence of various types of quality coffee, Balegede Village has great potential to become a center for coffee production. Through the 'Kopi Bringka' program, coffee farmers and UMKM actors will be given training and assistance in utilizing digital technology, from the planting process to product marketing. Thus, it is hoped that local coffee can compete in a wider market, both domestically and internationally.

This initiative also focuses on strengthening the branding and marketing of local coffee, which is the key to achieving the success of MSMEs. Through digital marketing tactics, coffee from Balegede Village can be better known and in demand by the community. By utilizing online platforms, business actors can not only expand the reach of their products, but also interact directly with consumers. This approach is expected to increase the competitiveness of local coffee products in an increasingly competitive market.

As part of the commitment to support local economic growth, the parties involved in the 'Kopi Bringka' program strive to make coffee from Balegede Village not just a product, but also part of the identity and pride of the community. By combining the potential of natural resources, creativity, and technology, it is hoped that this village will be increasingly known as one of the coffee centers in Indonesia.

5.3. Testimonials from MSME Actors

The success story of Bringka coffee entrepreneur.

Every region certainly has business potential that can be developed and become one way to encourage its people to progress. There are various types, even typical agricultural products if in creative hands can become unique, innovative and iconic products from a region. One of them is an innovation created by the people of Balegede Village, Naringgul District , Cianjur , West Java , Indonesia .

For a long time, the people in the area have been known for their profession as coffee and vetiver farmers. Both are indeed different ingredients, but when combined, they can become a beverage product with a distinctive taste. That product is Bringka Coffee.

He told about how the innovative idea initially emerged which became the main strength of his business cluster. Initially, he had income from Arabica Coffee, so there was a discourse to create new innovations from coffee and other ingredients. The idea had been around for a long time, but only started the processing business a few years ago.

The Kopi Bringka business cluster has grown into several business groups. Over time, this business cluster has had a positive impact on the welfare of the surrounding community. Even its management capacity has increased rapidly.

For the process of making Bringka Coffee, the business owner said that the process is almost the same as regular coffee, only involving 2 (two) stages, namely, the first is the coffee making process itself where after harvesting, the coffee beans are washed, dried and put into a *pulper machine* to be separated from the seeds. The second process is *roasting* and *grinding* until it becomes powder. After becoming powder, it is then mixed with other ingredients.

Meanwhile, coffee processing is also done in almost the same way. The beans that are harvested about once every 10-12 months are the beans, then washed until clean and dried. After that, the grinding process is carried out to make it powder so that it can be mixed with coffee powder. The entire process of making bringka coffee is carried out in a *greenhouse* located near the tourist village.

CHAPTER 6. FROM THE VILLAGE TO THE WORLD

6.1. Bringka Coffee Export Opportunities

Strategy for entering international markets.

Coffee in West Java has been proven to be able to penetrate the international market. This was proven in 2019, the export volume reached 0.36 million tons with an export value of USD 0.88 billion and production of 760.96 thousand tons. The coffee planting area in Indonesia is 1.26 million hectares, 95.45% of which is cultivated by People's Plantations (PR) while the rest is cultivated by Private Large Plantations (PBS) of 2.44% and state-owned large plantations (PBN) of 2.21%. Most of these coffee exports come from West Java, which is a large coffee producer and has been proven to contribute to the Indonesian economy. Coffee is one of the mainstay commodities that plays an important role in the economy in West Java Province. In 2020, the area of coffee plantations reached 45.2 thousand ha with a total production of 20.8 thousand tons. Based on ownership status, 99.5% or 45,183 ha are People's Plantations (PR), and the remaining 0.50% or 228 ha are privately owned plantations (Yusuf, ES, et al., 2022) .

The Kopi Bringka program not only focuses on producing high-quality coffee, but also seeks to create a village coffee brand that is able to compete in the global market. This aspiration reflects the hopes of Micro, Small, and Medium Enterprises (MSMEs) in Balegede Village to introduce the uniqueness of local coffee to the world. With an innovative digital approach, they hope to reach a wider consumer base and raise awareness of the quality and taste of the coffee they produce.

One of the important steps in building a strong village coffee brand is through strengthening product identity. By highlighting the unique characteristics and advantages of Balegede coffee, UMKM players can attract the attention of coffee lovers from various parts of the world. In addition, collaboration with various digital and e-commerce platforms is also expected to be an effective strategy to promote their products more widely. Through the use of social media, they can reach new markets and build a loyal coffee fan community.

However, to achieve this long-term vision, continuous support is needed from various parties, including the government, educational institutions, and the private sector. Support in the form of training, technical assistance, and promotion of local products will greatly influence competitiveness. With the synergy between MSMEs and other stakeholders, it is hoped that the quality and quantity of coffee products can continue to increase. This is important so that Kopi Bringka can not only become a local product, but also a proud brand on the international stage.

Along with the development of technology and the increasing public interest in local products, the hope of building a world-class village coffee brand is increasingly realistic. With the right efforts and sustainability, farmers and UMKM actors in Balegede Village can achieve the full potential of their local coffee.

Regulatory challenges and international standards.

While there are many benefits to achieving international standards, it also faces various challenges:

1. **Limited Resources**

Many MSMEs in Indonesia often face resource constraints, especially in terms of capital, labor, and technology. In the global market, demand for product quality and quantity is much higher than in the local market. Limited capital can hinder MSMEs from increasing their production capacity and product quality. In addition, the lack of skilled labor and advanced technology also hinders MSMEs from meeting international quality standards. To overcome this, collaboration with financial institutions or the government, such as through working capital loan programs or technical assistance, is essential.

1. **Rules and Policies**

Each country has different regulations and policies regarding product imports. For MSMEs, understanding and complying with these regulations is a big challenge. MSMEs must ensure that their products meet the health, safety, and environmental standards applicable in the destination country. For example, food or cosmetic products must meet certain health standards before they can enter a foreign market. For MSMEs that are not familiar with international regulations, this process can be time-consuming and costly. Therefore, support from related institutions to provide guidance in complying with regulations can be very helpful.

1. **Fierce Global Competition**

In the international market, MSMEs must compete with large companies from various countries that have larger production capacities and lower production costs. Products from countries such as China, which have high production efficiency, are often cheaper and more attractive to international consumers. MSMEs must strive to create added value to their products in order to compete in the global market. Innovation in design, use of environmentally friendly raw materials, or highlighting local uniqueness can be effective strategies to differentiate Indonesian MSME products from competitors.

1. **Logistics and Distribution Problems**

Logistics issues are one of the biggest challenges in exporting, especially for MSMEs that do not have experience in shipping products abroad. Slow or expensive shipping processes can reduce the competitiveness of MSME products in the global market. In addition, limited access to international distribution networks makes it difficult for MSMEs to reach customers in various countries. It is important for MSMEs to work with logistics companies that are experienced in international shipping to ensure that products arrive on time and in good condition. Governments and trade organizations can also help MSMEs by providing access to information on shipping rates and opportunities for wider distribution networks.

1. **Exchange Rate Fluctuations**

Currency exchange rate instability is another risk that needs to be anticipated by MSMEs who want to export. Exchange rate fluctuations can affect the selling price of products in the international market and ultimately affect business profitability. For example, when the rupiah exchange rate weakens against the US dollar, the price of export products can become more expensive for foreign buyers, potentially reducing the attractiveness of the product. To overcome this problem, MSMEs can consider using a hedging strategy to reduce exchange rate risk or work with banks that offer financial services for exports.

6.2. Inspiration for Other Villages

Case study of Balegede Village as a village development model.

Kopi Bringka's journey reflects the great potential of local Indonesian coffee, especially in the context of Balegede village. This movement has succeeded in empowering MSMEs by integrating the necessary innovations in every stage of production and marketing. By focusing on developing a variety of products, Kopi Bringka not only offers high-quality coffee, but also introduces various interesting flavors and experiences for consumers.

The implementation of digital marketing is one of the keys to success in optimizing the potential of the Indonesian coffee market. By utilizing digital platforms, local entrepreneurs in Balegede are able to reach a wider audience, both domestically and internationally. This digitalization allows them to compete with other coffee products in the global market, as well as increase the visibility and brand awareness of their signature coffee products.

In addition, the community spirit that is woven into this movement also strengthens the identity of local coffee. Every cup of coffee served by MSMEs in Balegede is not just a drink, but also contains local stories and culture that enrich the consumer experience. Efforts to promote Bringka coffee effectively must continue to be carried out, so that the success that has been achieved can continue and develop. Thanks to the cooperation between MSMEs, the government, and various stakeholders, the future of Indonesian coffee looks increasingly innovative and competitive. With a unique taste and a modern marketing approach, Bringka Coffee is ready to become the pride of the Indonesian people and can make achievements on the international stage.

Steps to replicate the mentoring program.

Mentoring is the process of accompanying and accompanying someone in a close, friendly, and brotherly manner. Mentoring can also be interpreted as an activity carried out by a social group, such as teaching, directing, or coaching.

Steps in replicating a mentoring program may include:

- Preparation
- Negotiation
- Empowering growth
- Closing

Some things that can be done in mentoring include:

- Get to know and introduce participants to each other

- Listening and asking questions in a facilitative manner
- Non-verbal communication
- Providing forward or feedback
- Managing his feelings and the feelings of the group
- Manage the game

6.3. Long Term Vision for Bringka Coffee

Continuous innovation in coffee processing.

Coffee product diversification is a strategic step that cannot be ignored by micro, small, and medium enterprises (MSMEs). In the context of MSMEs in Balegede Village, training on creative coffee processing is an important medium to introduce innovation in the use of coffee. In addition to beverage products, this training also touches on coffee-based snack products and coffee applications in the beauty industry. These creative products not only enrich consumer choices but also increase competitiveness in the market.

The use of coffee as a raw material in snacks such as cakes, cookies, or even healthy snacks, makes coffee more than just a drink. Creativity in creating coffee-based snacks can attract the attention of consumers who are looking for new alternatives. By combining the distinctive taste of coffee and quality ingredients, MSMEs can offer unique products that meet the increasing market demand for innovative snacks.

In addition, coffee exploration in beauty products is also starting to get attention. In this training, participants are taught how to process coffee into scrubs, face masks, or other skin care products. The benefits of coffee which are rich in antioxidants and anti-inflammatory properties make it an ideal ingredient for beauty products. By showing the added value of coffee in this sector, Balegede Village MSMEs can take advantage of opportunities in a market that is fond of natural-based products.

Overall, integrating various innovative coffee preparations not only helps MSMEs to attract a wider market, but also supports more effective marketing efforts. Product diversification is key to facing competition and expanding the reach of consumers who seek uniqueness in every product they consume.

Dream of making Bringka coffee a global icon.

Bringka Coffee, as a representation of local coffee from Balegede village, has great potential to gain attention in the global market. With the increasingly rapid growth of the coffee industry, the opportunities available for micro, small, and medium enterprises (MSMEs) in this village to innovate and compete are increasingly wide open. This strategy will not only improve the quality of the coffee it produces, but also educate consumers about the uniqueness of Bringka Coffee.

To build a global village coffee brand, it is important for MSMEs in Balegede to implement sustainable farming practices. This includes the use of organic methods and processing techniques that maintain the distinctive taste of Bringka Coffee. In addition, collaboration with research institutions and universities can provide farmers with access to the latest training and knowledge in the field of coffee farming. This also allows MSMEs to innovate in coffee-based products, such as ready-to-drink coffee or other processed products that can increase added value.

The use of digital technology also plays a crucial role in expanding market reach. Through e-commerce platforms and social media, UMKM players can market Kopi Bringka to various consumer segments, both domestic and international. This also provides an opportunity to build a community of coffee enthusiasts that focuses on local products. The hope is that this community will not only be consumers, but also spread information and stories about the uniqueness of Kopi Bringka.

With these strategic steps, it is hoped that Kopi Bringka can become a village coffee brand that is not only known domestically, but also internationally. Through innovation, collaboration, and utilization of technology, the future of Kopi Bringka can shine brighter, making it one of the leading products from Balegede village that is worthy of being considered in the global market.

CHAPTER 7. CONCLUSION AND RECOMMENDATIONS

7.1. Conclusion

The mentoring program has shown positive results so that it can be maximized, the mentoring program is not only carried out seasonally but must be continuous and scheduled. Thus, what has been taught by the community service actors is truly absorbed and can be applied under the supervision of the mentoring officers who supervise activities related to coffee problems.

The role of technology and innovation in village development is very important. Current technology is inseparable from coffee management starting from planting, maintenance and harvesting. The process of making coffee from raw materials to ready to serve requires adequate technology. That is why further training is needed specifically for coffee farmers so that coffee products are of higher quality and durable so that when sold they can remain of high quality. Innovation is also needed to create variations of coffee products with various flavors and aromas that are increasingly demanded by coffee lovers.

7.2. Recommendations for Related Parties

The recommendations in this report for universities, government and relevant MSMEs are as follows:

University: Higher Education Institutions, in this case Universities, must further enhance the role of the Tri Dharma of Higher Education, especially the Dharma of Community Service, continuously and on schedule to maximize mentoring programs for UKMK coffee farmers.

Government: The government should increasingly support village-based innovation policies by providing facilities and permits to community service actors in higher education environments.

MSMEs : MSMEs are increasingly collaborating for business sustainability with universities, government and other related parties such as market players, traders and coffee exporters to improve the development of coffee MSMEs in the relevant villages.

7.3. Hope for the Future

Village potential as an innovation-based economic driver: Regarding the potential of villages as an economic driver through MSMEs, its level of importance is no longer in doubt. This was once stated by the Minister of Finance, Mrs. Sri Mulyani, that the development and empowerment of Micro, Small, and Medium Enterprises (MSMEs) is very important for the global economy because MSMEs are the backbone of the world economy. Micro, Small, and Medium Enterprises (MSMEs) are one of the Foundations of the National Economy, based on data from the Ministry of Cooperatives and Small and Medium Enterprises, the contribution of MSMEs reaches 99% of all business units, contributes to GDP of 60.5% and is able to absorb 96.9% of the workforce. Micro, Small and Medium Enterprises (MSMEs) have emerged as one of the vital pillars of the Indonesian economy. MSMEs have proven to be resistant to crises, even becoming *boosters of* economic recovery during the crisis.

The role of local products in building Indonesia's reputation in the world. Local coffee products have reached the global market. One of the agricultural sectors that can drive the development of social and economic welfare is coffee plantation farmers. It can be said that coffee is a superior commodity because its market opportunities are quite good in both domestic and foreign trade (exports). Coffee commodities in Indonesia have an important role as a source of non-oil and gas foreign exchange for the country from the agricultural sector. Indonesia is the fourth largest coffee producer in the world, so there is a great opportunity for each region to manage environmental assets as a source of economic drivers. Since 2019, the volume of coffee exports has reached 0.36 million tons with an export value of USD 0.88 billion and a production of 760.96 thousand tons. Most of these coffee exports come from West Java, which is a large coffee producer and has been proven to contribute to the country's economy. Thus, coffee has become an important mainstay commodity in the economy in West Java. Furthermore, in 2020, the area of coffee plantations in West Java reached 45.2 thousand ha with a total production of 20.8 thousand tons. Based on ownership status, 99.5% or 45,183 ha are People's Plantations and the remaining 0.50% or 228 ha are privately owned plantations (Yusuf, ES, et al., 2022).

Attachment

Data and statistics related to the mentoring program .

Meetings were held 8 (eight) times. Meeting 1 opening. Meetings 2 to 7 main events of community service activities. Meeting 8 closing.

Photo documentation of mentoring activities.

Yess
Kopi Asli Balegede
KOPI BRINGKA
Arabika
Natural
Robusta
Honey
Wine
Kiwos
PREMIUM
100 gram
150 gram
200 gram
Diproduksi:
LMDH Balegede
Dikemas:
BUMDes karya Binangkit

A practical guide to implementing technology in MSMEs.

Some practical things that can be used for implementing technology in

SMEs include:

First, Create digital bookkeeping.

The uses of bookkeeping are: 1) Planning 2) Evaluation 3) Knowing the number of transactions 4) Decision making 5) Knowing the amount of profit/loss 6) Tax calculation 7) Knowing the amount of assets, capital, debts 8) Cost control 9) Information for management 10) Easy to get bank loans

To do digital bookkeeping with the BukuKas application, the following features are used:

1. Transaction features that present transaction data per day, per week or per month,

2. Financial report features that can help to obtain profit and loss reports, accounts receivable reports and customer reports,

3. The record feature functions to record total sales and total expenses,

4. Accounts receivable feature that records accounts receivable transactions in detail so that payments are well controlled.

5. Digital business card features make it easier for business people to promote their business to customers,

6. Multi Book feature that manages financial transaction bookkeeping records from several businesses being run,

7. BukuKasPay feature is a payment feature to make it easier for users to make payments on various platforms, such as Bank Virtual Accounts, QRIS and popular e-wallets such as OVO, DANA, GoPay, LinkAja, and ShopeePay.

Steps to use the Cash Book Application

1. Download the BukuKas application on the Play Store or App Store
2. After that, enter the mobile phone number used for business. Then, the BukuKas application will send an OTP number to your smartphone. You can choose this OTP number, whether you want it sent via SMS, WhatsApp, or phone. After receiving and entering the OTP code, you will enter the main page
3. Input sales transactions by:

- Click the "Add Transaction" button on the smartphone screen
- Then, enter the price of the goods or products you sell today in the "Sales Nominal" column. Let's say the price of Chicken Rice you sell is Rp. 50,000 per portion. Then enter the number Rp. 50,000 in the sales nominal
- The number written here is the capital you spend to make one portion of Chicken Rice. For example, your capital is Rp. 20,000. The application will automatically calculate. Next, you will see a slide button that says "Paid" and "Not Paid". If your buyer has paid in full, then the slide button is towards "Paid
- The next step you can enter the details of the goods you sell. For example, the specifications of the Chicken Rice you sell are Rica-rica Chicken Rice. Then enter the menu in the item details. You can also add the amount, if the buyer buys more than one.
- If so, the next step is to choose the payment method used by your buyer. Whether transfer, cash, credit, and so on.
- Before saving the transaction, first enter the contact alias name of your buyer so that the transaction data you have is more complete. No need to enter the cellphone number, you can just write the name, it doesn't matter.
- If so, immediately click "Save Transaction". Later, you will be thrown to the next page that shows the invoice for the transaction. You can send this invoice to customers via WhatsApp, email, social media, and so on.

1. Input expense transactions by:

- Click the "Add Transaction" button on your smartphone screen. Select "Expenses."
- Enter the nominal amount of expenditure and complete the data on what costs were incurred/paid, for example transportation costs amounting to Rp. 100,000.
- Next, click "Save Transaction" and you're done.

1. Record accounts receivable by:

- Open the "Accounts Payable" menu then select "Add Accounts Payable" on the smartphone screen
- Select "Give" to record receivables, or "Receive" to
- Next, click "Save Transaction"
- Click the calendar symbol to set the payment due date.
- Select "Save" and you're done. The due date serves as a reminder of when the debt/receivable must be paid off.

1. View, Share & Download Reports:

- Enter the "More" menu then select "Download report"
- Specify the desired "Period" "Report Type" and "format".
-) Next, select "Download" or "Share" the Report, and Done.

1. Create a "DIGITAL BUSINESS CARD" by:

- Enter the "Other" menu then select "Business Card"
- Complete the data to create a business card, then "Save"
- After that, the business card can be "Shared" and/or "Downloaded" by the user (Source: https://panduan.bukukas.co.id)

Second: Creating Digital Marketing on Tokopedia

To create digital marketing on Tokopedia, use the following steps:

1. Open the Tokpedia website: https//www.tokpedia.com

2. Look for the Register link then click on the link.

3. Fill in the account registration section using the cellphone number or email you already have and click register if it is filled in.

4. Select Confirm or verify your account from Tokopedia via the options provided by the Tokopedia system. Then enter the secret code from

Tokopedia that has been sent via cellphone or email.

5. Fill in your Tokopedia account name completely. Then click the finish button.

6. After you have finished registering, don't forget to fill in the security PIN code so that your account is extra protected.

7. Re-enter the confirmation code received from adding the extra PIN code from the previous step on Tokopedia.

8. Once completed, the account will look like this:

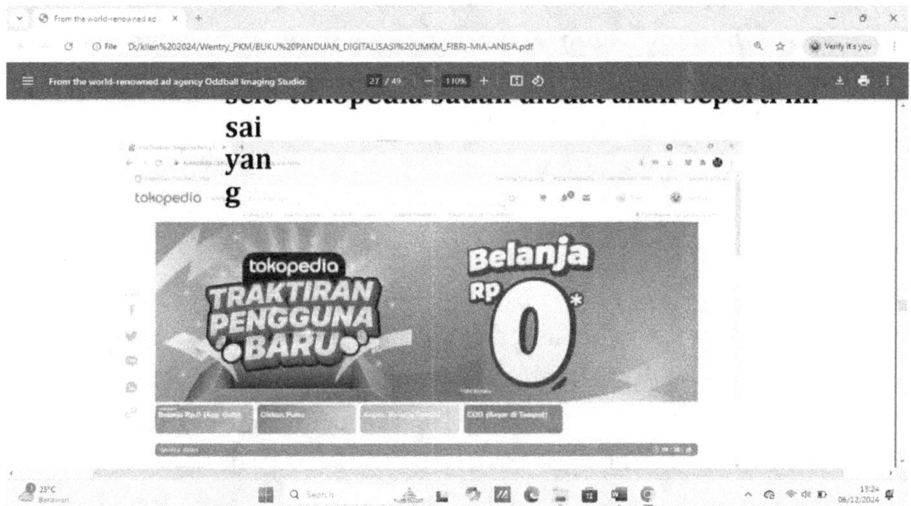

9. Click on the account name section to fill in the biodata and other details completely.

10. Fill in your personal data completely and in accordance with your personal data. In your personal data, list your address, payment details if any and your bank account so that it can be used for withdrawals.

11. Click on the address list, then click on add new address. After that, fill in the new address according to your ID card, starting from the address label

to the address, then click add.

12. Click on the bank account, then click the Add Account button again, then fill in the name of the bank you want to add. Then fill in your account number again according to the name of the bank you have, then click save.

13. Next, you return to the main page by clicking on the Tokopedia label at the top left, then click on the shop at the top right and click again to open the shop.

14. Fill in the cellphone number, shop name, then domain or website and your shop address and click save if everything has been filled in and matches your personal data.

15. Next, scroll or go down to the left and look for settings. Then click on your store settings and your store screen.

16. Still in the information section, then you scroll or go down again and you will be shown the shop status section and please fill in the shop status by clicking on the shop operational page and don't forget to include a picture of your shop under the shop status.

17. The next step, you are asked to click on the notes section, then click add notes and add shop policies according to your shop's terms and conditions, then click save.

18. The next step, you are asked to click on the location section to fill in your shop location, then you click on the add shop section and fill in the sections starting from Andi's location label to tax, then click save.

19. The next step, you click on the delivery section then you determine the origin of your delivery, after that you scroll or go down to look at the delivery service section to fill in the delivery service.

20. Next, you select the delivery service available in your area, and click the check mark on the delivery service you want, then click save.

21. Next, click on the service section, to activate the service if you want it by clicking the tick on the I agree section then click activate service. If you don't want it, activating the service is also not a problem.

22. Next, you click on the Tokopedia seller section. Then you look for the product section and then click add product to sell online on the left side of the Tokopedia website.

23. Next, you fill in the add product section and upload or send a photo of your product.

24. Next, you scroll or go down again to fill in the product information section starting from the product category name to the display that matches the product you want to sell.

25. Next, you scroll or go down again, you fill in the details of your product starting from the condition, product description and video of the product you want to sell.

26. Next, you scroll or go down again, you fill in the product variant section by clicking add. Then you fill in the price section again starting from the minimum order, unit price and wholesale price.

27. Next, you scroll or go down again, you fill in the product management section, by filling in the product status, product stock and SKU.

28. The last step, you fill in the weight and shipping section starting from the product weight, product size, shipping insurance, shipping service and finally pre-order if you want then click save (Fibriyan NK)

Bibliography

Alfonsus Jefri Oematan (2024), Rancang Bangun Mesin *Roasted* Biji Kopi Timor Portable

Ahmad Fachrurozi (2023). Manfaatkan Teknologi Digital Untuk Tingkatkan Daya Saing UMKM. News BSI

Amos, D., Au-Yong, C. P., & Musa, Z. N. (2021). The mediation effects of finance on the relationship between service quality and performance of hospital facilities management services. Facilities. https://doi.org/10.1108/F -12- 2020-0130

Berbasis *Internet of Things* (IOT) dengan Mikrokontroler ESP 32. Jurnal Krisnanda, Vol. 3 No 3.

Cicea, C., Popa, I., Marinescu, C., & Ştefan, S. C. (2019). Determinants of SMEs' performance: evidence from European countries. Economic Research-Ekonomska Istrazivanja, 32(1), 1602–1620.

Chen, L., Ellis, S. C., & Suresh, N. (2016). A supplier development adoption framework using expectancy theory. International Journal of Operations & Production Management, 36(5), 592–615. https://doi.org/10.1108/IJOPM-09- 2013-0413

Dewi Meisari Haryanti (2022), Potensi Ekspor Produk Kopi. UKM Indonesia

Desa Mulyadadi (2023). Pelatihan Manajemen untuk Meningkatkan Kinerja UMKM

Dwi Erianto (2023). Komoditas Kopi: Sejarah, Manfaat, Produsen Dunia, Produksi, Sentra

Produksi dan Ekpor Indonesia. Kompas Media

Fibriyan NK (2021) Digitalisasi Bisnis Sederhana bagi UMKM. Universitas Mulawarman.

Fitriani, F., Ismono, H., & Rosanti, N. (2011). Produksi Dan Tataniaga Beras Di Propinsi Lampung. JSEP (Journal of Social and Agricultural Economics), 5(1), 1-11.

Fitriani, S., Unteawati, B., & Widyawati, D. K. (2019). Polinela Smart Market-Place untuk Penguatan Jejaring Kluster Rantai Pasok dan Bisnis Berkelanjutan Polinela Smart Market-Place for Streghthen Sustainable Supply Chain Network. In Prosiding Seminar Nasional Pengembangan Teknologi Pertanian IPTEKS (pp. 1-10).

Gunday, G., Ulusoy, G., Kilic, K., & Alpkan, L. (2011). Effects of innovation types on firm performance. International Journal of Production Economics, 133(2), 662–676. https://doi.org/10.1016/j.ijpe.2011. 05.014

Hess, J., & Story, J. (2005). Trust-based commitment: multidimensional consumer-brand relationships. Journal of Consumer Marketing, Vol. 22, 313-322. https://doi.org/10.1108/073637605 10623902

Humas Tel-U Surabaya (2023). Peran Teknologi Informasi dalam

Meningkatkan Efisiensi Bisnis Logistik. Telkom University Surabaya.

Hogan, S. J., & Coote, L. V. (2014). Organizational culture, innovation, and performance: A test of Schein's model. Journal of Business Research, 67(8), 1609– 1621. https://doi.org/10.1016/j.jbusres.2 013.09.007

Kaleka, A., & Morgan, N. A. (2017). Which Competitive Advantage(s)? Competitive Advantage–Market Performance Relationships in International Markets. Journal of International Marketing, 25(4):25-49. https://doi.org/1 0.1509/jim.16.00 58

Kemenkop-UKM. (2020). Peraturan Menteri Koperasi dan Usaha Kecil dan Menengah Tentang Rencana Strategis Kementerian Koperasi dan Usaha Kecil dan Menengah Tahun 2020-2024. kemenkopukm.go.id, Juni 29. https://kem enkopukm.go.id/uploa ds/laporan/1602751704_Permen %20KUKM%20N omor%205%2 0Tahun%202020%20tentang%20 Renstra%20Kementerian%2 0Ko perasi%20dan%20UKM%20Tah un%202020-2024.pdf. (diakses pada, 24 Februari 2022).

Kemenkop-UKM. (2021). TARGET PEMERINTAH 30 JUTA UMKM MASUK EKOSISTEM DIGITAL PADA TAHUN 2024. kemenkopukm.go.id, Juni 02. https://kemenkopukm.go.id/read/t arget-pemerintah-30-juta-umkmmasuk-ekosistem-digital-padatahun-2024. (diakses pada, 24 Februari 2022).

Khaeroni (2018). Kehidupan Sosial Ekonomi Petani Kopi di Desa Kadindi Dompu. Jurnal Humanitas, Vol. 5 No. 1

Kim, S., Kim, B., & Seo, M. (2020). Impacts of Sustainable Information Technology Capabilities on Information Security Assimilation: The Moderating Effects of Policy— Technology Balance. Sustainability, 12(5). https://d oi.org/10.3390/su121561 39

Kotler, P., & Keller, K. L. (2012). Manajemen Pemasaran. PT Indeks.

Leppe, E. P., & Karuntu, M. (2019). Analisis Manajemen Rantai Pasokan Industri Rumahan Tahu di Kelurahan Bahu Manado. Jurnal EMBA: Jurnal Riset Ekonomi, Manajemen, Bisnis Dan Akuntansi, 7(1).

Lima tantangan Ekspor Bagi UMKM: Memahami Kendala dan Membangun Solusi Untuk Keberhasilan Global (2024). Linkumkm

Malepati, V., Latha, C. M., & Nageswararao, K. S. (2021). Determinants of

Access to Finance by MSMEs in Andhra Pradesh. SEDME (Small Enterprises Development, Management & Extension Journal), 48(2), 203-219. https://doi.org/10.1177/09708464 211066630

Marcelino Rivaldi, dkk (2022). Analisis Manajemen Rantai Pasok Komoditas Kopi di Desa Liberia Kabupaten Bolang Mangondow Timur. Jurnal EMBA, Vol. 10 No. 2

Membangun Desa Berkelanjutan: Mengenali dan Menerapkan Penguatan Ekonomi Kreatif berbasis Komunitas (2024). Panda

Meningkatkan Manajemen dan Keberlanjutan: Pengembangan UMKM di Desa melalui Program Pendampingan dan Pelatihan (2024). Panda

Novta & Sumiyana (2023). Analisis Kebutuhan UMKM Dengan Menggunakan Pendekatan Penalaran Hieraraki Maslow Secara Organisasional. Accounting and Business Information Systems Journal, Vol 11 No 3.

Osano, H. M., & Languitone, H. (2015). Factors influencing access to finance by SMEs in Mozambique: case of SMEs in Maputo central business district. Journal of Innovation and Entrepreneurship, 5(1). https://doi.org/10.1186/s 13731- 016-0041-0

Pulka, B. M. (2021). Entrepreneurial competencies, entrepreneurial orientation, entrepreneurial network, government business support and SMEs performance. The moderating role of the external environment. 28(4), 586–618. https://doi.org/10.1108/JSBED-12- 2018-0390

Ratna, dkk (2022). Analisis Rantai Pasok (*Supply Chain*) Kopi Robusta di Kabupaten Lampung Barat.

Siaran Pers Kementrian Koordinator Bidang Perekonomian Republik Indonesia, HM.4.6/591/SET.M.EKON.3/10/2022

Sekariyanti Wilasasri (2021). Pentingnya Inovasi Teknologi Terhadap Peningkatan Produktivitas Pertanian. LPM Nuansa

Sumardi, & Fernandes, A. A. R. (2020). The influence of quality management on organization performance: service quality and product characteristics as a medium. Property Management, 38(3), 383–403. https://doi.org/10.1108/ PM-10- 2019-0060

Sureshchandar, G. S., Rajendran, C., & Anantharaman, R. N. (2002). The relationship between service quality and customer satisfaction— A factor specific approach. Journal of Services Marketing, Vol. 16, pp 363-379. https://doi.org/10.1108/088760402 10433248

Stoll, E. E., & Ha-Brookshire, J. E. (2012). Motivations for Success: Case of U.S. Textile and Apparel Small- and Medium-Sized Enterprises. Clothing and Textiles Research Journal, 30(2), 149-163. https://doi.org/10.1177/0887 302X1 1429740

Tripathy, S., Aich, S., Chakraborty, A., & Lee, G. M. (2016). Information technology is an enabling factor affecting supply chain performance in Indian SMEs: A structural equation modelling approach. Journal of Modelling in Management, 11(1), 269–287. https://doi.org/10.1108/JM2-01- 2014-0004

Vij, S., & Bedi, H. S. (2016). Are subjective business performance measures justified? International Journal of Productivity and Performance Management, 65(5), 603–621. https://doi.org/10.1108/IJPPM-12- 2014-0196

Wilden, R., Gudergan, S. P., & Nielsen, B. B. (2013). Dynamic Capabilities and Performance: Strategy, Structure and Environment. Long Range Planning, 46(1–2), 72–96. https://doi.org/10.1016/j.lrp.2012.1 2.001

Yusuf, E.S., dkk., (2022) Sustainability Strategy and Business Model of Arabica Coffee in West Java: A Case Study in Garut Regency. Analisis Kebijakan Pertanian, Vol. 20 No. 1

Yoga. A Musika (2023). Clod Brew Adalah Variasi Minuman Kopi Semua Kalangan. Otten

Seputar Hobi (2023). Mengenal Teknik Cold Brew dalam Menyeduh Kopi

Zhou, K. Z., Brown, J. R., & Dev, C. S. (2009). Market orientation, competitive advantage, and performance: A demand-based perspective. Journal of Business Research, 62(11), 1063–1070. https://doi.org/10.10 16/j.jbusres.20 08.10.001

https://teknobringka.store/kegiatan-pendampingan-kopi-bringka-men ingkatkan-kreasi-produk-olahan-kopi-umkm-desa-balegede-berbasis-tek nologi/

www.ingramcontent.com/pod-product-compliance
Lightning Source LLC
Chambersburg PA
CBHW071549260726
48653CB00007BA/2603